GW00758797

'KNOW THE GAME' SERIES

WRESTLING

Produced in collaboration with
the National Technical Committee of
THE BRITISH AMATEUR WRESTLING ASSOCIATION

CONTENTS

796.812/GC 591

GARDA SIOCHÁNA
07641
Library Services
Headquarters Inspectorate

GARDA SIOCHÁNA COLLEGE
LIBRARY
TEMPLEMORE, CO. TIPPERARY.

Price

INTRODUCTION

WRESTLING, which originated in ancient Greece, is one of the oldest-known sports. It is one of the finest forms of exercise, bringing into use all the muscles of the body, and is also a wonderful mental stimulant. Moreover, it is one of the compulsory sports of the present-day Olympic Games, where two forms are practised: freestyle and the Greco-Roman style.

With freestyle wrestling, which has evolved from the Lancashire and "catch-as-catch-can" styles, any fair hold is allowed, but in the case of the Greco-Roman style no holds are allowed below the waist and the use of the legs is not permitted. Two other styles are practised in Great Britain: the Cumberland and Westmorland and the Devon and Cornwall. This book deals only with freestyle wrestling.

The National Amateur Wrestling Association was formed in 1904, the name being changed to the British Amateur Wrestling Association in 1945. The Association is affiliated to the International Amateur Wrestling Federation under whose rules all competitions, matches, championships, Olympic Games, Asian Games, Empire and Commonwealth Games, and international matches are conducted.

Four associations are affiliated to the British Amateur Wrestling Association: the Eastern, Western and Midland Counties Association, the Northern Counties Association, the Southern Counties Association and the Scottish Amateur Wrestling Association.

Each of the four associations holds county and counties championships in junior, intermediate and senior grades. Every year from the counties championships, two wrestlers are nominated in each of the weights to enter the British Open Championships, which are organised by the British Amateur Wrestling Association.

For the junior grade of wrestler, there are three distinct weight categories; 10, 14 and 17 year age groups. Schoolboy wrestling is controlled in England by the Schoolboy Olympic Wrestling Association and in Scotland by the Scottish Amateur Wrestling Association.

With the intermediate grade the age group is from 17 to 19 years, and a wrestler enters the senior grade when he is over 19. Weights are the same for both these grades and are given in the section on international rules at the end of the book.

Wrestling takes place on covered mats 9 metres in diameter with a padded surround of from 1·20 m. to 1·50 m. to obviate injury from contestants falling outside the mat area.

Intermediate and senior wrestling bouts are each of nine minutes' duration: three periods of three minutes with a minute rest between. Junior wrestling bouts are of six minutes' duration: two periods of three minutes with a minute's rest between.

GARDA SIOCHANA COLLEGE TEMPLEMORE LIBRARY

A wrestling bout is controlled by a referee, time-keeper and one judge. A fall is given when a wrestler holds both the shoulders of his opponent to the mat for a period of one second; the referee counts one, striking the mat with his hand at the same time. For a fall to be valid, the judge must agree with the referee. Each of the wrestlers wears a coloured costume, one red and the other blue.

If no fall occurs, the judge's score sheet is handed to the mat chairman who declares the result of the bout.

During the bout the referee signals the points scored with the thumb and first two fingers (1, 2, 3 or 4) held aloft with the colour of the wrestler scoring. The referee wears a coloured sleeve, red on one arm and blue on the other arm. The judge records the scores on his score sheet, and holds aloft a coloured plaque, red or blue, with the numbers 1, 2, 3 or 4 of the wrestler scoring the points as they occur.

The scoring points given to a wrestler for various moves are given in the section on international rules.

This book has been produced by the Technical Committee of The British Amateur Wrestling Association, to further amateur wrestling as a recreational and competitive sport. The holds and throws described are the basic ones given to beginners in the sport. A number of publications on advanced wrestling can be obtained from booksellers.

WRESTLER'S OUTFIT

Fig. 1

A wrestler's outfit consists of a costume, jock strap, wrestling boots, socks, track suit and handkerchief.

HOLDING HANDS

WRONG

Fig. 2

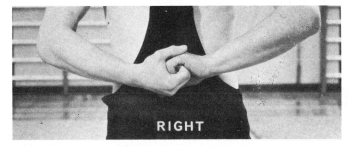

RIGHT

Fig. 3

When hands are clasped during wrestling the fingers must never be interlaced as shown in Fig. 2; the Butcher's Grip (Fig. 3) must be used.

Fig. 4

Wrestling stance

WRESTLING STANCE

The stance of a wrestler is very important. The most suitable and strongest position is with the feet well apart and in line, the knees bent and loose, the body leaning forward from the hips, the hands up and the elbows well in at the sides (Fig. 4).

The position described is in no way stiff; stiffness causes slowness of movement, loss of agility and speed. In wrestling, speed is of enormous importance. Keeping the feet well apart makes for stability, a broadening of the base of the figure the wrestler represents. Narrow that base by bringing the feet close together and loss of balance will result.

Fig. 5
Initial hold

INITIAL HOLD

The usual method of engaging with an opponent is by the initial hold (Fig. 5). The right hand is placed behind the opponent's neck, the left forearm is placed in the crook of his right arm (this permits you to ward him off if he advances, by applying your closed hand to his chest) and the forehead is placed against his shoulder. From this hold many take-downs and throws can be executed.

STANDING THROWS

Fig. 6

Fig. 7

Cross-buttock throw

From the initial hold, slip your left arm down, grasping your opponent's right arm, and move your right arm from his neck to his right shoulder, at the same time pivot on your left foot, turning into him (Fig. 6) with your buttocks well into and under him. Now pull with both arms, fetching your opponent over the lower part of your back (Fig. 7) and finally drop on to your right knee, bringing him down on his back (Fig. 8). Practise the various stages slowly until the movements are right. The throw itself must be completed in a fast, continuous movement.

Fig. 8

Fig. 9   Fig. 10   Fig. 11

Leg pick-up and back heel

From the initial hold, bring your right arm from your opponent's neck and grasp his arm, at the same time stepping to his right side and grasping his right leg with your left arm (Fig. 9). Now lift his leg and as you do so place your right leg behind his left leg (Fig. 10). Lastly sweep his left leg away with your right leg and bring him to the mat (Fig. 11).

Fig. 12

Fig. 13

Double thigh pick-up

From the initial hold, move your left hand from under your opponent's right arm to a position above his elbow, forcing his arm upwards (Fig. 12). Now drop quickly, grasp his thighs (Fig. 13) and lift (Fig. 14). From this position drop on to your right knee, keeping hold of your opponent's right leg, grasping his body with your right arm and bringing him down (Fig. 15).

9

Fig. 14

Fig. 15

Fig. 16

Fig. 17

Fig. 18

Further arm and near leg pick-up

From the initial hold, push your opponent's right arm (which is holding your own neck) upwards with your left hand; pass under his arm to his right side, retaining your right hand hold of his neck and pulling downwards (Fig. 16). Then, with your left hand, lift his near leg (Fig. 17), and by dropping on to your right knee put him on his back (Fig. 18).

Fig. 19

Fig. 20

Cross ankle take down

From the initial hold, retain your right hand hold on your opponent's neck and with your left hand take hold of opponent's left ankle (Fig. 19). Now drop on to your right knee, at the same time pull opponent's left leg towards you and pull with your right arm bringing him to the mat (Fig. 20).

Fig. 21

Fig. 22

Flying mare throw

From the initial hold, release your grip on your opponent's neck, pivot on your left foot bringing your right arm under his right armpit and hold his upper arm firmly (Fig. 21). Retain your hold with the left hand while completing your turn. To enable you to get right under your opponent's armpit you will have to bend your knees slightly. Note that at the finish of your turn, your back will be to your opponent (Fig.

Fig. 23

22). Now maintain your hold on your opponent's right arm and drop to your right knee, at the same time leaning forward and pulling hard on his arm, so allowing him to come over your shoulder. You should remain on your knee and let your opponent fall in front of you (Fig. 23), releasing your left hand as he touches the mat. Immediately grasp his head and pull it towards his right shoulder (Fig. 24) so reducing his chances of bridging out of danger.

Fig. 24

Fig. 25

Fig. 26

Fig. 27

Standing arm roll

From the initial hold, release your grip on your opponent's neck and bring your arm smartly across his head (Fig. 25), securing his right arm tightly, turning in with your buttocks against him and at the same time stretching your right leg backwards (Fig. 26). Now drop on to your knee, at the same time rolling to your right and keeping a firm hold of your opponent's arm, thus bringing him to the mat (Fig. 27).

Lancashire turn

This movement is one that enables you to get behind your opponent from the standing position.

From the initial hold, release your hold on your opponent's neck, bring your right arm over his head (Fig. 28), reach down and grasp the inside of his right thigh and press down on his right shoulder and arm (Fig. 29). Now bring your right foot forward, pivot on it and bring your left foot right round behind your opponent, grasping him round the waist. Make sure your legs are far enough away to prevent your opponent grasping your feet or legs by bending and reaching through his legs (Fig. 30).

Fig. 28

Fig. 29

GROUND DEFENCE POSITION

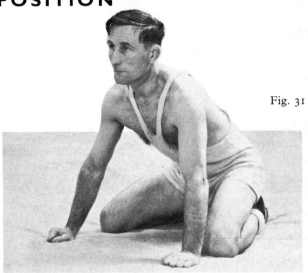

Fig. 31

Fig. 30

Fig. 31 shows the usual position a wrestler tries to adopt when he is brought down to the mat. He sits back on his heels with his arms outstretched, his hands clenched, his knees apart and his back straight, making a strong base against attack. In this position, the fingers are never outstretched with the palms resting on the mat.

GROUND CONTROL POSITION

Fig 32

Having brought your opponent to the mat, you consolidate the move by holding him round the waist with your right arm, your right hand being placed against the inside of his right thigh, your left hand grasping him just above his left elbow, and your right knee against his left foot (Fig. 32). From this position you are in control and can make a number of moves.

GROUND POSITION

Fig. 33

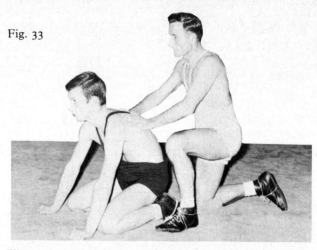

When two wrestlers are brought to the centre of the mat to restart a bout after it has been interrupted, the position shown in Fig. 33 is always adopted. The 'underneath' wrestler must adopt the ground defence position; the 'top' wrestler must place both his hands on his opponent's shoulder-blades. The 'top' wrestler can kneel on one knee, both knees, or can even stand, but he cannot resume wrestling until he hears the referee's whistle. The object of this is to prevent a surprise attack being made.

GROUND THROWS

Quarter Nelson

From the ground control position, bring your left forearm across the back of your opponent's neck and, with your left hand holding his right shoulder, force his head down with your forearm, at the same time putting your right arm through under his left arm and grasping your own wrist (Fig. 34). Now release your hand from his shoulder, grasp his head and pull it towards your right knee (Fig. 35), keeping your shoulder well under your opponent's body, which enables you to push with your shoulder at the same time as you pull his head towards you, thus turning him over on to his back (Fig. 36). To obtain a fall in this way, a tight hold must be maintained when the opponent is brought over, the weight of your body being pitted against him and your legs being kept well stretched out.

Fig. 34

Fig. 35

Fig. 36

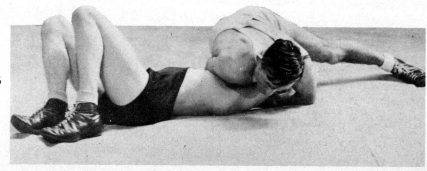

Fig. 37

Fig. 38

Half Nelson

From the ground control position, with both hands on your opponent's neck, force his head down (Fig. 37) and place your left arm under his near arm and across his head (Fig. 38), at the same time bringing your right arm under his body and holding, with your right shoulder well under him (Fig. 39). As in the previous hold, you pull his head towards you, push with your shoulder and lift with your right arm, forcing him over on to his back, and keeping your weight on him to obtain a fall.

Fig. 39

Fig. 40

Further Nelson

From the ground control position, bring your right
arm under your opponent's right arm, place your left
arm across his neck (Fig. 40) and join your hands by
the Butchers Grip (see Fig. 3); then force your
opponent's head down with your forearm. When his
head is on the mat, pull your right hand through with
your left hand (still maintaining the Butchers Grip)
to the near-side of your opponent's head (Fig. 41).
Lastly, with your right arm, force your opponent over
on to his shoulders (Fig. 42).

Fig. 41

Fig. 42

Fig. 43

Fig. 44

Further Nelson and arm

From the ground control position, keep hold of your opponent's forearm, place your head against his armpit and force him forwards and down (Fig. 43). Keeping hold of his arm, bring your right knee up to it, at the same time placing your right arm under his right arm and round his head (Fig. 44). Now pull his head away from you and exert pressure with your right arm, thus bringing him over for a fall (Fig. 45).

Fig. 45

SIOCHANA COLLEGE LIBRARY TEMPLEMORE, Co. TIPPERARY.

Double Nelson

This is the one wrestling hold in which the legs must not be used and in which pressure must be applied sideways and not directed downwards. Bring your right arm under your opponent's right armpit and your left arm under his left armpit, join hands with the Butchers Grip and force his head sideways towards your right knee (Fig. 46); now force him forwards, keeping a tight hold to obtain a fall (Fig. 47).

Under no circumstances must you restrict the movement of your opponent's legs; otherwise he will not be able to turn over and may be seriously injured. This is a most punishing hold and is NOT ALLOWED in junior wrestling.

Fig. 46

Fig. 47

24

Fig. 48

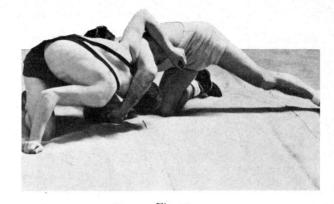

Fig. 49

Cradle hold

From the ground control position, the left arm is brought to the further side of the opponent's head and the right arm is placed round his left thigh (Fig. 48). Now join your hands with the Butchers Grip and force your opponent down on to his shoulder (Fig. 49); then lift with your right arm and bring him over for a fall (Fig. 50).

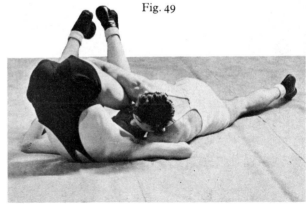

Fig. 50

Further arm hold

From the ground control position, grasp your opponent's right arm above the elbow with your left hand and force his arm upwards (Fig. 51); then, holding him tightly, bring your right arm through under his left arm, grasp his right shoulder (Fig. 52) and force him over on to his back to obtain a fall (Fig. 53).

Fig. 51

Fig. 52

Fig. 53

Ground Lancashire turn

This is a movement which enables you to get behind your opponent from the underneath ground control position. When your opponent's hold on your left arm, while in the control position, is released, immediately swing out into a sitting position, at the same time reaching back and grasping the inside of his right thigh (Fig. 54). Now press hard with your back against your opponent, rise up on your feet and swing round on top of him (Fig. 55), using your arm and his thigh as a pivot on which to get behind him. For this movement to be successful it must be executed very quickly.

Fig. 54

Fig. 55

Arm roll

When an opponent makes the mistake of getting his
weight too far over you, and the opportunity arises,
trap his right arm with your right arm and, holding
his wrist (Fig. 56), bring your right knee up close to
your left knee, roll towards your right and spin round
on top of your opponent (Fig. 57).

Fig. 56

Fig. 57

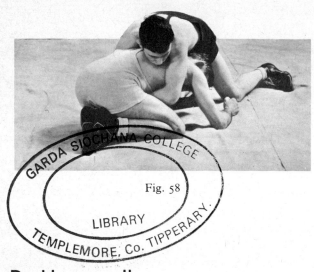

Fig. 58

GARDA SIOCHANA COLLEGE
LIBRARY
TEMPLEMORE, Co. TIPPERARY.

Fig. 59

Double arm roll

If, while working in front of you, an opponent makes
the very bad mistake of lying over you with both his
arms round your body (Fig. 58), immediately trap his
arms above the elbow (Fig. 59), holding them tightly;
then push against him to induce resistance and turn
either to the right or left, bringing him over with his
chest to your back and his back to the mat and keeping
his arms securely locked (Fig. 60).

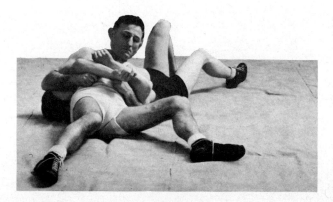

Fig. 60

EXERCISES FOR THE WRESTLER

Skipping, running and general physical exercises are very beneficial to wrestlers. But the most important exercises of all are those that come under the collective term 'bridging'. A strong neck is of paramount importance in wrestling and bridging exercises are aimed at its development.

Bridging exercises

1. Put your hands behind your back and rest your forehead on the mat with your legs apart; now rock backwards and forwards on your head (Fig. 61).

2. Take up the bridge position and rock backwards and forwards on your head, trying to touch the mat with your nose (see Fig. 62).

Fig. 61

Fig. 62

Fig. 63

Bridging exercises (*continued*)

3. Two wrestlers participate in this exercise. One stands and holds out his left forearm; the other holds the former's forearm with both hands (Fig. 63) and drops back into a bridge, his partner steadying him down (Fig. 64). After a little practice, a wrestler can drop back on his own.

Fig. 64

EXTRACTS FROM THE GRECO-ROMAN
AND FREESTYLE INTERNATIONAL WRESTLING RULES

Article 1—The definitions contained in the International Wrestling Rules shall be applicable to all Olympic Games competitions, world championships, Continental championships, international and regional competitions and to all international meetings. These definitions of the international rules shall likewise be applicable to all competitions organised by national federations which are members of the I.A.W.F.

Weight Classes

Article 2—International weight classes for Olympic Games competitions, world championships and international matches shall be as follows:

Kilos	Lbs.
48	105.82
52	114.64
57	125.66
62	136.69
68	149.91
74	163.14
82	180.78
90	198.42
100	220.46
over 100	

A competitor may compete in one class only, i.e. in the one corresponding to his own bodily weight at the time of the official weighing in, in any one competition. However, he may opt for the class immediately above should he have entered in this.

The final list of competitors shall necessarily be handed in before the weighing-in, in conformity with the regulations in force.

Article 3—On the first day of a competition, the weighing-in shall begin four hours before and end three hours before the first bout. On the following days, this formality shall begin two hours before and end one hour before the first bout.

In the case of competitions in which the number of contestants is more than 150, the International Technical Committee may alter the times for the weighing-in, the drawing of lots and the pairing-off.

In the case of competitions in which the programme lasts for several days, contestants shall be weighed each day. Wrestlers who have fought their last bouts one day before the end of the competition shall not be weighed on the last day, this to apply to all weight classes.

Competitors shall be weighed-in nude and, before the weighing-in, shall be examined by doctors (one of whom shall be the doctor appointed by the organising country); the latter shall refuse all those who present any danger of contamination. Competitors must be in satisfactory physical condition.

Their nails shall be cut very short and shall be examined at the weighing-in.

Until the end of the weighing-in, competitors shall have the right to get on the scales as many times as they wish, but each in his turn.

Dress

Article 6—Competitors shall appear before the public in a one-piece singlet and under this they shall wear a truss or a suspender-belt.

The singlet shall be tight-fitting and shall cover the body from the middle of the thighs upward; it shall not be cut away by more than two palm-widths around the neck and arms.

The use of light knee-guards shall be permitted.

Nothing whatsoever may be added to this dress, save in the event of a stoppage of the bout on account of injury or for any other reason, when the wrestlers may cover themselves with a warm garment.

The use of shoes with heels or with nailed soles shall be forbidden; contestants shall likewise be forbidden to cover their bodies with greasy or sticky products and they shall not be in a perspiring condition.

No bandages shall be allowed on the wrists, arms or ankles, save in the case of injury and on the doctor's prescription.

The wearing of rings, bracelets, buckle-type shoes and all objects liable to injure an opponent shall likewise be forbidden.

Each competitor shall be freshly shaven at the time of the weighing-in.

Each competitor shall be provided with a handkerchief.

Each competitor shall be given two anklets with a width of 10 centimetres and of the colour attributed to him (red or green). Competitors shall be forbidden to wear shoes, socks and laces coloured green or red or with a colour close to green or red.

The Mat

Article 7—A mat having a diameter of 9 metres surrounded by a border of the same thickness and with a width of from 1·20 to 1·50 m., is obligatory in all international competitions.

On the inside of the circle of 9 m. in diameter, and running all along its circumference, a 1 metre wide band of red colour is traced, this being an integral part of the wrestling surface.

To designate the various parts of the mat, the following terminology will be employed.

—The interior part of the mat inside the red band will be called: Central Wrestling Surface (7 m. in diameter)

—The red band: passivity zone (width 1 m.)

—The border: protection surface (width 1·20 to 1·50 m.).

Fig. 65
Layout of equipment and officials' positions for a wrestling tournament.

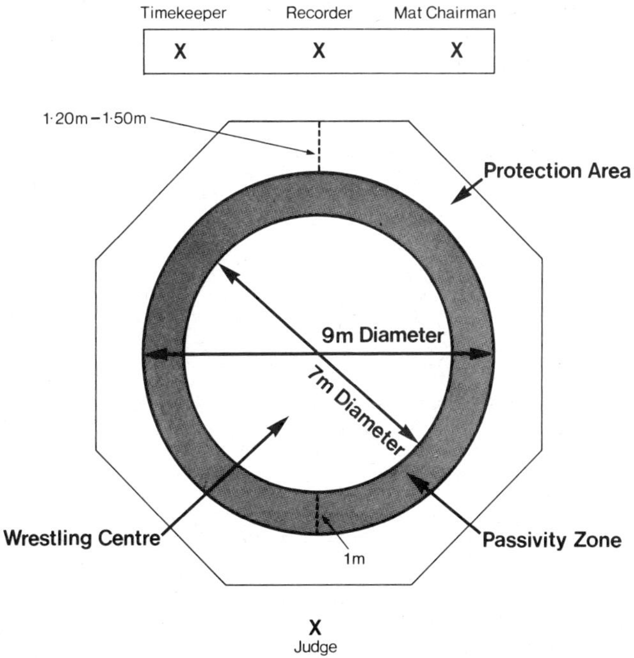

Timekeeper   Recorder   Mat Chairman

X   X   X

1·20m – 1·50m

Protection Area

9m Diameter

7m Diameter

Wrestling Centre

1m

Passivity Zone

X
Judge

Referee, Judges and Adjudication Board

Article 10—In all international competitions, the officials for each bout shall consist of one mat chairman, one referee, and one judge.

The changing of a judge during a bout shall be forbidden.

In order to avoid all partiality, compatriots of the competitors may not be a judge; the same shall apply in the case of the referee.

The referee shall be responsible for the evolution of the bout, which he shall control in conformity with the rules. The bout shall start, be interrupted and end when he blows his whistle. He alone shall be authorised, after consulting the judges, to give cautions. He alone shall order the wrestlers to return to the mat should they have left it, or order the bout to be continued in the standing position or on the ground, with the respective opponents in the on-top or underneath positions, this with the approval of the majority of the judge.

The referee and the judge shall be dressed in white and they shall wear the badges of their countries.

The judge and referee shall assume all the duties, prerogatives and responsibilities provided for in the rules for

35

international wrestling competitions, by the interpretations included in this appendix, by the regulations of the Technical Committee and by the regulations for the organisation of competitions.

It shall be the duty of the referee and the judge to follow the bout with attention, from beginning to end, and to judge the actions in such a way as to ensure that the result shown on their forms shall exactly reflect their general impressions.

The duties, prerogatives and responsibilities of the judge shall also be as follows:

be entitled to cause the timing device to be stopped or to stop the bout.

Each bout shall last until the opponent has been defeated. If this defeat occurs before the elapse of the maximum time laid down, a win shall be recorded, to be counted as a fall, and the bout shall thereupon end.

The timekeeper shall call out the times in a loud voice every minute, in French, English and the language of the organising country.

The Start and Duration of the Bout

Article 11—The duration of each bout shall be nine minutes in both styles, this being divided into 3 periods, i.e. of three minutes.

After the first and second period of wrestling, a break of one minute shall be given.

Whenever a contestant endeavours to hold up the contest (by lacing his shoes, going off the mat, etc.), the referee shall ask for the timing device to be stopped.

The referee alone, acting upon his own conviction, shall

Article 12—Should a competitor fail to put in an appearance on the mat after his name has been duly called, he shall be considered as having lost by a fall and shall be eliminated from the entire competition.

A tolerance period of five minutes shall be allowed in the case of acceptable reasons, but this only for the first bout in the first round for each class.

Before the bout, the opponents shall take up their positions in opposite corners of the mat; the referee shall place himself in the middle of the mat and shall call the two wrestlers to his side in order to examine their dress and to verify the fact that they are not covered with any greasy or sticky product and that their hands are bare.

The wrestlers shall greet each other, shake hands and then go to their espective places, each place being marked in the same colour as that of the anklet already given to each contestant, which they must necessarily keep on until the result of the bout has been announced. When the referee blows his whistle, the two wrestlers come together and start wrestling immediately. They do not have to shake hands again until the end of the bout.

Article 13—A bout may begin, be interrupted or end only on the blowing of the referee's whistle. No competitor shall be entitled to decide for himself that his opponent shall be sent back from the edge of the mat to the middle.

The Stopping of the Bout

Article 14—At the end of the first and second periods, both wrestlers shall be sent back to their respective corners.

Foul holds

Article 22—The pulling of hair, flesh, ears, private parts and singlet shall be forbidden. The twisting of the fingers and toes shall be forbidden. Brawling, kicking, throttling, pushing and the applying of holds liable to endanger the life of an opponent, or cause a fracture or dislocation of his limbs, shall likewise be forbidden.

Holds intended to torture one's opponent or to cause him to suffer pain, so that he will be compelled to give up, shall likewise be forbidden.

Stepping on an opponent's feet shall be forbidden.

The touching of an opponent's face between the eyebrows and the line of the mouth shall be forbidden. The gripping of the throat shall be forbidden.

In the case of holds applied in the standing position and from behind, when the opponent is turned with his head pointing downwards (inversed waist hold), the throw shall be made solely to the side and not downwards (head-first pike); part of the body, other than the feet, of the contestant who is applying the hold must touch the mat before the upper part of the body of the contestant who is being attacked does so.

A bridge must be pressed down, i.e. it shall be forbidden to lift one's opponent when he is in the bridge position and then throw him down on the mat (severe impact with the ground); it shall likewise be forbidden to cause a bridge to collapse by pushing in the direction of the head.

The double head-hold (double Nelson) shall be permitted; however, the hold must always be applied from the side, without the legs being used in any way against any part of the opponent's body.

The bending of an opponent's arm through an angle of more than 90 shall likewise be forbidden.

Head holds using both hands shall be forbidden. When a hold is being applied, the holding of the head shall be allowed using one arm only.

It shall be forbidden to force one's elbow or knee into the opponent's abdomen or stomach.

An opponent's arm may not be forced behind his back in such a position that his forearm and arm form a closed angle and with a pressure being applied at the same time.

Head-locks shall be forbidden no matter how they are applied.

Contestants shall be forbidden to speak to each other during the bout.

FOUL HOLDS—GRECO-ROMAN WRESTLING

It shall be forbidden to seize one's opponent below the hips or to grip one's opponent with one's legs.

All pushing, pressure or lifting made with the legs when in contact with a part of the opponent's body shall be forbidden.

It shall, for example, be forbidden for the attacker, while wrestling is in progress on the ground, to lift his opponent by using his legs against his knee and thigh in order to secure a fall.

FOUL HOLDS—FREESTYLE WRESTLING

Tripping and sideways striking with the feet or legs shall not be forbidden.

Scissors grips applied with the legs to the head or body shall be forbidden.

It shall not be necessary to accompany one's opponent to the ground when applying certain holds with the foot.

The gripping of an opponent's singlet shall be forbidden and clinging to the mat shall likewise be forbidden, both in freestyle wrestling and in Greco-Roman.

Placing in Danger

Article 23—It shall be considered that a wrestler is in a position involving a "placing in danger" when he goes beyond the vertical line by 90° with his back turned towards the mat and resists with the upper part of his body to avoid being placed in a position in which both of his shoulders are on the mat (the fall).

The wrestler may resist with his head, elbows and shoulders.

A placing in danger shall be counted when:

(a) The wrestler who is defending forms a bridge in order to avoid a fall.

(b) The wrestler who is defending has his back towards the mat and is resting on one or both elbows.

Passive obstruction

Article 26
Continual obstruction of the holds of the active contestant,
Wilful running off the mat,

Continual lying down flat on the stomach, and the fact of holding both the opponent's hands, with a view to preventing him from engaging the combat, shall be considered as passive obstruction.

Article 27—No special points shall be awarded for activity, and activity shall not be a factor in the decision as to whether the bout has ended in a win.

Article 28—In the case of a moving off the mat, the contestant at fault shall be given a caution, *but the referee must make certain that the contestant was not pushed off by his opponent;* in addition, the referee shall explain to the wrestler at fault the reason for this caution.

Interruption of the bout

Article 29—Should a contestant be obliged to interrupt the bout as a result of nose bleeding, a fall on the head or any other acceptable reason beyond his own control, the referee shall suspend the wrestling for a maximum of five minutes in one and the same bout.

This stoppage may be allowed in one or more periods up to a total time of five minutes for each wrestler; if these five minutes are exceeded for one and the same wrestler, the bout may not be continued; however, the injured wrestler shall be notified of the end of the period of tolerance.

Should a serious mistake be made by the judges or the referee, the mat chairman shall intervene and shall stop the bout by sounding the gong; after consulting the referee and the judge, he shall give a ruling with regard to the difference.

Scoring

Article 30—The judge shall mark the wrestlers' points on their scoring forms as follows:

1 point: (a) to a wrestler who brings down his opponent and holds him on the ground by getting on top;

(b) to a wrestler who reverses his opponent and holds him down;

(c) to a wrestler who applies a correct hold and does not cause his opponent to touch the mat with either his shoulder or head during the execution of the hold.

A caution shall count as one point to the opponent.

2 points: (a) to a wrestler who applies a correct hold and places his opponent momentarily in danger (less than five seconds);

(b) to a wrestler whose opponent is in an instantaneous fall, accidental fall, or rolling fall.

3 points: (a) to a wrestler who keeps his opponent in danger (the shoulders forming an angle of less than 90° with the mat) for five seconds.

A series of rolling falls and bridges for five seconds, continuously, will count for three points. In this case, the referee shall count the seconds.

The judge shall mark down the points as and when they are awarded in each period.

When the difference between the two opponents is less.

4 points: for a perfect Technical throw.

than one point, the bout shall be declared a draw.

Should the number of points awarded to both wrestlers be equal, the winner is the wrestler with the first Technical Point. There should be no draws.

Should there be a difference of one or more points, the winner shall be the contestant who has the larger number of points.

To ensure a uniform marking, the actions which have resulted in the fall shall not be marked down on the scoring forms, but only the earlier actions. The mere marking down of the word "fall" shall indicate final action.

The mat chairman also marks down points on a scoring form.

The Fall

Article 31—Defeat by reason of a fall shall be pronounced if there is a three-vote decision in accordance with the table given in the appendix to these regulations.

It will be a fall when both shoulders are in contact with the mat for the count of 1 signified by the referee hitting the mat with his hand once.

For a fall on the edge of the mat to be recognised as valid, it shall be sufficient for the contestant's head and both shoulders to touch the mat at the moment of the fall.

A fall shall be valid provided the judge makes no observations. Should there be a conflict of opinions the mat chairman decides.

A win on points

Article 32—Should there be no fall within the nine minutes laid down for the duration of the bouts in both styles, the judge shall hand in his scoring form to the mat chairman and he shall name the winner or decide that the bout has been drawn.

Complete rules can be obtained from:
B.A.W.A., 60 Calabria Road, London, N.5.

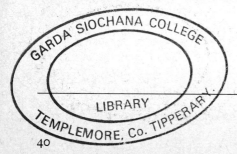
GARDA SIOCHANA COLLEGE LIBRARY TEMPLEMORE, Co. TIPPERARY

Printed in Great Britain by John S. Speight Ltd. Guiseley, Leeds